The Story of Corn

by Mary Lindeen

Consultant:
Adria F. Klein, PhD
California State University, San Bernardino

CAPSTONE PRESS
a capstone imprint

Wonder Readers are published by Capstone Press,
1710 Roe Crest Drive, North Mankato, Minnesota 56003.
www.capstonepub.com

Books published by Capstone Press are manufactured with paper
containing at least 10 percent post-consumer waste.

Library of Congress Cataloging-in-Publication Data
Lindeen, Mary.
The story of corn / Mary Lindeen. — 1st ed.
    p. cm. — (Wonder readers)
Includes index.
ISBN 978-1-4296-7971-8 (paperback)
ISBN 978-1-4296-8641-9 (library binding)
1. Corn—Juvenile literature. 2. Corn—History—Juvenile literature. I. Title.
SB191.M2L56 2012
633.1'5—dc23   2011022003
Summary: Simple text and color photos explain what corn is, how it's grown,
how it's been used in the past, and how we use it today.

Note to Parents and Teachers

The Wonder Readers: Social Studies series supports national social studies
standards. These titles use text structures that support early readers, specifically
with a close photo/text match and glossary. Each book is perfectly leveled to
support the reader at the right reading level, and the topics are of high interest.
Early readers will gain success when they are presented with a book that is of
interest to them and is written at the appropriate level.

Printed in the United States of America in North Mankato, Minnesota.
102011   006405CGS12

Table of Contents

Ears and Stalks

Peel back the leaves on an **ear** of corn, and you will find a tasty surprise. Inside the **husks**, there are rows and rows of yellow **kernels**. These corn kernels grow out of an inner core called a **cob**.

Ears of corn grow on the stalks, or stems, of the corn plant. Long thin leaves grow on the stalks. A corn stalk is a big plant. It can grow to be over 8 feet (2.4 meters) tall.

Corn Long Ago

People have been eating corn for thousands of years. It used to grow wild in North and South America. It was a very important food for the people living there. American Indians learned how to plant and grow corn, which they called **maize**.

They used it in their cooking in many different ways. They would grind it up into cornmeal. They dried corn kernels and later cooked them into a kind of mush. They also figured out how to heat kernels until the kernels popped into popcorn.

The first people from Europe to come
to America had never heard of corn.
American Indians showed the settlers
how to grow and cook corn. In fact,
it was one of the foods served during
the first Thanksgiving feast.

The settlers had to figure out how to grow enough food in their new land to keep their families from starving. Corn became an important crop. It grew quickly, there were many ways to cook it, and it could be stored through the winter.

Corn Today

Corn chips and corn cereal are foods made out of cornmeal. People also use cornmeal to make corn bread and corn dogs. When you eat pizza, there might be cornmeal on the bottom of the crust. It keeps the pizza from sticking to the pan.

Corn syrup is a sweet liquid made from the natural sugars in corn. Corn syrup is used to sweeten juice, soda, and other snack foods. Some things we use around the house are made from corn too, such as drinking straws and garbage bags.

Of course, people also eat corn right off the cob. The kind of corn we eat this way is called sweet corn. You can buy sweet corn kernels in a can or frozen in a bag, or you can buy whole ears. It is a healthy vegetable no matter how you fix it.

Corn is also used as feed for animals. It is usually mixed with other grains and vitamins to keep farm animals healthy. Some people put out corn to feed squirrels and birds in the winter.

Growing Corn

Farmers plant corn in the spring. It grows all summer long. Hot, humid weather is just what corn needs. As the stalks push up out of the ground, leaves begin to unroll. Then ears grow on the stalks. Thin, brown strands of corn silk come out of the top of each ear.

Tassels grow at the top of each stalk. The tassels have **pollen** on them. Pollen falls down onto the corn silk. Each piece of silk is attached to one kernel on the ear of corn. By fall, the corn silk will be dry and brown. The kernels inside the husks will be juicy and ripe. The corn is ready to **harvest**.

Corn is grown in more countries than any other crop. It is eaten by people all around the world. Buy some corn the next time you are at the grocery store or the farmers' market. It is a healthy and tasty way to eat your vegetables!

Now Try This!

Create a "corn collage" by gathering labels of food and other products that are made with corn. You could also cut out pictures of items from magazines or print computer images of corn products. You may be surprised to find out how many things you eat and use every day that contain corn.

Glossary

cob   the middle part of an ear of corn on which corn kernels grow

corn syrup   a sweetener made from corn

ear   the part of a corn plant where the seeds grow

harvest   to pick or gather a crop

husk   the part of a plant that covers the fruit or the seeds

kernel   a grain or seed, especially of corn

maize   corn; the corn plant

pollen   tiny grains of flowering plants that help the plant make seeds

Internet Sites

FactHound offers a safe, fun way to find Internet sites related to this book. All of the sites on FactHound have been researched by our staff.

Here's all you do:

Visit *www.facthound.com*

Type in this code: 9781429686419

And go to Capstonekids.com for more about Capstone's characters and authors. While you're there, you can try out a game, a recipe, or even a magic trick.

 **Super-cool stuff!** Check out projects, games and lots more at **www.capstonekids.com**

Index

Editorial Credits

Maryellen Gregoire, project director; Mary Lindeen, consulting editor; Gene Bentdahl, designer; Sarah Schuette, editor; Wanda Winch, media researcher; Eric Manske, production specialist

Photo Credits

Alamy: North Wind Picture Archives, 9; Bridgeman Art Library International: Peter Newark Pictures/ Private Collection/C. W. Jefferys, 8; Capstone Studio: Karon Dubke, 1, 7, 10, 11 (all), 12, 15, 16; Corbis: PoodlesRock, 6; Shutterstock: DenisNata, 5, Inacio Pires, cover, James Horning, 13, rsooll, 14, Zeljko Radojko, 4

Word Count: **583**   Guided Reading Level: **L**   Early Intervention Level: **20**